For Mavis

No Homeless Problem
And Other Poems

By Séamus Fox
From the Stories of the Homeless

I hope you
enjoy these poems,

Séamy

No Homeless Problem
And Other Poems

Building futures, Bridging divides

No Homeless Problem
And Other Poems

By Séamus Fox
© Séamus Fox

ISBN: 9781912092550

First published in 2018 by Arkbound Ltd (Publishers)
Cover by Jonathan Plumb

Arkbound is a social enterprise that aims to promote social inclusion, community development and artistic talent. It sponsors publications by disadvantaged authors and covers issues that engage wider social concerns. Arkbound fully embraces sustainability and environmental protection. It endeavours to use material that is renewable, recyclable or sourced from sustainable forest.

Arkbound
Backfields House
Upper York Street
Bristol BS2 8QJ
England

www.arkbound.com

Dedication

In memory of
David Joyce,
Our Companion.

"My homeless heart has
made a beggar of me
and I can't seem
to panhandle even
a penny's worth of
love from your pockets."

Jessica Katoff
Poet and novelist

"People are needed to take up the challenge,
strong people, who proclaim the truth,
throw it in people's faces,
and do what they can
with their own two hands."

Abbé Pierre
Founder of Emmaus

Contents

Acknowledgments

Ali Hill
Les Jevins
Terry Waite
Jo Andrews
Steve Davis
Lyn Watson
Clare Hunter
James Hayes
Vanessa Daly
Jennie Farrell
Jessica Foster
Karen Brown
Steve Jackley
Steve Jackson
Matthew Last
Colin Hassard
Jessica Hodge
Selwyn Image
Cathy Hembry
Tara Constable
Amanda Stekly
Katie Silvester
Jonathan Plumb
Diane Docherty
Mimi O'Halloran
Kelly Thompson
Debbie Chessum
Kelly-Louise Meacock
and everyone at Emmaus

Forward

By Terry Waite

I am often asked what, if anything, I gained from spending
many years as a hostage. Then I thought the time was totally
wasted but now, looking back across the years, I realise that
I was learning a great deal.

For most of my life I have had sympathy for those who
found themselves on the margins of life: prisoners, captives,
the disadvantaged. During those years my sympathy was
developed into empathy. Sympathy is to feel sorry for others.
Empathy is to feel as they feel. Now I know what it is like to
be deprived of family, friends and the many things in life
that most of us take for granted.

On my release I was asked to assist in the development of
Emmaus in the UK, a unique organization working to enable
the homeless to develop their dignity as human beings and
live a full and purposeful life. During the past 26 years I
have met hundreds of formerly homeless people who have
entered an Emmaus community and I have listened to their
stories. Most people never have an opportunity to hear the
authentic voice of the homeless. The stories are told by
people from every walk of life, from those who have had a
professional career to those who have had little education.

In this remarkable collection of verse, Séamus Fox, who was
homeless himself, tells movingly of his own experiences and
the experiences of other homeless people whom he has met.
Some, like Séamus, eventually found their way to Emmaus
and to a fuller life. Some did not. He chooses his words

carefully and in concise language that conveys something of the agony of isolation.

Anyone who may have casually dismissed the homeless as being parasites should read what Séamus has written. It is insightful, moving and compelling. The writer has the gift of language and is able to put into verse the feelings and aspirations of many. This is a unique book written by a compassionate man.

Terry Waite, September 2017

Author's Dedication

There are many opinions about what Emmaus is from many people, most of whom know nothing substantial about it aside from what they hear or assume. I know one thing about it above all else. If this organisation did not exist there would be thousands of people whose lives would have much less meaning and probably tens or hundreds of people who would be dead.

This book is my contribution to Emmaus because I have spent the last two years coming to know the joy of normality in communities that shouldn't really work, but that somehow do. If Emmaus had not existed I have no idea what would have happened to me when I became homeless. I only know that my life now is so much easier and more fulfilling because of this amazing organisation.

Séamus Fox, November 2017

Introduction

From January to November of 2017, I made round trips of more than 1600 miles combined across England to compile these 71 poems from the testimonies of 44 previously homeless individuals.

These poems will disturb and enlighten, they will disgust and empower. There is laughter and great sadness here; there is death and life, there is nothing and there is everything. These poems reflect not individuals but society. These poems highlight the inevitability of a social order that allows so many of its subjects to go without love and basic necessities, then later further punishes these individuals when they become mentally and emotionally disturbed as a result of never having known normality or been properly versed in love and respect.

I sat down with these amazing people and they spilled themselves onto me. This is an unnervingly honest collection. I listened intently as these people spoke to me then formed the poems using the words they uttered, framed in the structure I taught myself over three decades while I furiously tried to understand myself and the world around me through writing.

I wrote this book because I want people who have never been homeless or who have never known homeless people to search in their souls for shreds of compassion. Homelessness is not a choice, it is an inevitability brought about by social and economic factors creating unjust pressure, generation after generation for people whose burdens come from being born to disadvantaged mothers and fathers at the wrong end of an upended game in a greed-driven excuse for civilisation.

Please open your minds and your hearts for the purpose of understanding because no one who is suffering or who is creating suffering is choosing to live like that. People do not choose their feelings. The twisted adults of today were made that way in dark childhoods. Until we care for and love and respect and feed and empower EVERY child, then we will always create the next generation of damaged adults in neglected childhoods while society looks the other way pretending it did all it could.

Séamus Fox, November 2017

Vulnerable

I remember the
5th of November.
I found a bin-shed to
stay in for the night.
I was cold so I drank
a half bottle of vodka
to warm myself up
before going to sleep.
Some kids heard me
snoring and thought
it would be funny to
throw lit fireworks in
through the door slats.
As they ran away with
regardless laughter
I woke half-traumatised
amid echoing explosions.
I felt very vulnerable so
I had to move elsewhere
but I could never find
anywhere comfortable
because comfortable
is a state of mind.

I loved to play similar
pranks when I was
younger but it seemed
different because I was
alone, hopeless and
unhappy.

Hot Chocolate

Constantly sitting
on the pavement
without the comforts
that many people
take for granted
can be so tough that
normality becomes
a distant concept.
One harsh winter's
night, a woman and
her mother came and
sat with me, they cared
enough to do that at least.
She was not like the
others, she had been
homeless once herself
and the compassion in her
eyes told me she understood.
They didn't stay long but
it was long enough for me
to feel a warm connection.
She bought me a burger
and some hot chocolate.

The combination of the
freezing night and our brief
connection made it the
most awesome hot
chocolate I have ever
tasted in my life.

Estranged

Years of excessive
drinking and erratic
behaviour meant
I became estranged
from my mother
and my family for
more than a year.
One restraining order
later, I walked the streets
alone, full of guilt and
regret, with a level of
sadness that I had never
known and that I have
never known since.
The police often came
to check up on me and
one day they told me
that my mother might
see me at some point
but it would better for
me to wait for her to
initiate the contact.

I couldn't wait, I went to
her door, my old home.
She answered and half
jokingly asked me what
I was doing there, then
she allowed me in and
I was humble enough
that we could begin to
rebuild our relationship.

A Scarf

I was sleeping in a
park and a woman
who was walking her
dog there came and
asked if I was alright,
asked if I had eaten.
I hadn't had much to
eat that day so she
directed me to a café
and told me to wait
there until she arrived.
When she came to meet
me, she sat and talked
to me, she treated me
like a person, she got me
some food and a cup of
tea and gave me a scarf.
I kept the scarf and I
remember her by it.
People are not all bad.

Cautious

After months of
staying with friends
I eventually had to
admit that I was an
actual homeless person.
I went to a day centre
in my home town.
I was only in there ten
minutes waiting for
someone to notice me
when a young man came
in an extremely agitated state,
clothes blackened, hair singed.
He had been sleeping in
a wheelie bin that someone
had set alight and he was
probably lucky to be alive.
I was about to start sleeping
rough at that point and
I decided it would be better
to find isolated areas outside
the town than risk being
burned to death.

Pillbox

There used to be
an old World
War II Pillbox
down by the
canal that I
often slept in.
I didn't make
a home there
but I liked going
there and relaxing
with my wind-up
radio and a candle.
When you don't
have much you
learn to appreciate
the little things
you do have.
Eventually my
life changed
and I moved on,
but any time
I went back to
that part of the
world, I would
go and see my

old Pillbox.
I think you should
never forget where
you came from or
you can more
easily end up
going back there.

Denial

I was very angry,
I didn't know why.
After arguments
with my mother
and stepfather
I found myself
alone without
a place to live.
I got a flat but
I couldn't handle
my finances so I
was evicted, yet
I never considered
myself to be a
homeless person.
I didn't know any
homeless people
and I didn't beg,
so how could
I be a homeless
person? I stayed
with friends when
I could and I often
walked about all
night drinking because

there was nothing
else to do at the time.
When you're in a bad
situation sometimes
it's easier to deny it
than to face the truth.

Mind

Slowly I began
to realise that
my mind was
not as ordinary
as I would have
liked it to be.
Dissatisfaction
and depression
became normality
and as I went further
into the depression,
I became suicidal.
I began to see a fear
in the eyes of my
supposed friends,
this meant I was
no longer welcome.
Soon I was so out
of control that I
had lost everything.
I didn't become
homeless because
of alcohol or drugs
or financial woes.

I became homeless
because I lost my
mind and control
of my emotions.

Slugs

It was summer.
I was sleeping in
the woods away
from the world and
my fear of people.
I woke one sun lit
morning dying for a
drink so I reached
out for the half can
of Special Brew
from the night before.
There was a big slug
just beginning to make
its way up the can and
I thought I was lucky
to have caught it
before it got in there.
I brushed it off then
took a massive swig
only to have my throat
greased with a horrible,
thick mucus like goo
that was once a slug.

I then wretched for
ages making the most
disgusted noises.
It is difficult to imagine
that anything could
make Special Brew taste
worse but a disintegrated
slug will do just that.

10 Days

I only knew
him for 10 days.
We were teenagers.
At the hostel
we were staying
in, an older man
with a heroin
habit told us how
we could make
seventy quid a week
getting a methadone
script and selling it.
All you needed was
some needle marks.
I didn't want to get
involved but my
new friend went
the next morning.
That night I went
to his room and he
was laid on the bed
like a heroin cliché:
a needle in his arm,
he was very dead.

It was the first time
he had tried drugs.
I only knew him
for 10 days.

No Homeless Problem

The white-headed
right wing-politician
announced on the
news that there was
no homeless problem.
I would see soup runs
nightly for 100 plus
people, but there was
no homeless problem.
I had no home so I
would wash and eat
often in day centres
and I would shelter
in bookmakers' shops
until they closed but
still they said there was
no homeless problem.
In the harsh winters we
would get news of the
ones who had died on
the streets yet still they
kept saying that there was
no homeless problem.

Change

Before I was
homeless I was
a very successful
businessman and
I had a deeply
cynical attitude
towards those who
were on the streets.
I thought they were
all junkies and
alcoholics and that
all of their misery
was a result of their
own poor life choices.
Some years later during
a particularly harsh
winter on the street
I pondered the difference
between what I was and
what I had become.
We don't notice change
happening, usually we
only know about it
when it has changed
beyond all recognition.

Saviours

After arriving
in this country
other people's
plans had changed
and that meant
I was homeless.
I presented myself
as such at the
council offices but
they told me there
was a waiting list
of thousands and
they wouldn't be
able to help me.
A woman who was
volunteering there
overheard my plight
so she and her husband
gave me a room for
the weekend and
later helped me to
get somewhere
more permanent.

If she hadn't been
there I would have
been sleeping on
the streets.

Not a Choice

I was trying to
explain to her that
not all homeless
people drink.
She couldn't fathom
that, I could see it
in her confused eyes.
She had an idea that
every single person
who ever became
homeless was a raging
alcoholic with tatty
clothes and terrible
unhygienic habits.
I told her that I had
met lots of homeless
people and that many
of them drank normally
and some never drank.
In one sense I thought
she was ignorant but in
another I knew that
her ignorance was
not a choice.

Nearly

For a time I was
wandering not
knowing where
I was going or
what I was doing.
When the mind is
unsettled life can
become a void
without purpose.
One night I bought
a bottle of vodka
and walked to the
cliffs at the coast
half intending
not to come back.
As I sat there staring
out into the sea
waiting for something
an old woman came
along and told me
not to do it, she said
she could see the
death in my eyes.

She took me to her
house, made me
some food and she
talked to me as
if I was a person.
I stayed the night in
her spare room then
I left the next morning.
I have never seen her
since, it was like she
was there just when
I needed someone.

Thermals

I was selling
the *Big Issue*
when a man
gave me £20
for myself.
I went to a
camping shop
and bought a
decent set of
winter thermals.
I was thankful
that he had given
me the money
to buy them.
I was still on
the streets but
when you're out
there it is the
little things
that you come
to appreciate.

The kindness of
strangers really
makes a difference
when you're freezing,
struggling to survive.

Nowhere

There was trouble
inside of me but
alcohol and drugs
were the only things
that made feelings.
I didn't get along
with my mother's
new boyfriend so
she sent me with
no return ticket to
my father, away
in the cold North.
He didn't want me
either so he sent
me back, one way.
I didn't know where
to go and I ended up
in a town between
the two, alone, having
been rejected by the
people who made me.
I sat on a bench with
all of my belongings,
watching a busker.

He noticed me and
came to speak to me
asking me what was
wrong and how I ended
up sitting there with
all of my possessions.
He was genuine and
generous, he gave me
the money he had
made for that day,
there was £60 in all.
As night came, he left
and I sat there alone
wondering what was next.

Prophecy

When I was
about seven
or eight, my
family would
go on holidays
to the coast.
My mum told
me that I would
always stop and
stare at homeless
people in the street.
I wouldn't speak,
I would just look
at them, no doubt
wondering what
was wrong there,
wondering why
they were different.
More than three
decades later I
became homeless,
and I often wonder
if I was staring
because I felt some
kind of affinity

with those people.
Did my younger self
know something
that I would not know
until much, much later?

Peoples Feet

Sometimes I would
be so exhausted that
I wouldn't be able
to even think and I
would just sit on the
pavement watching
passing people's feet.
There was always this
fear that I had to push
to the back of my mind
because I had to keep
going and maybe those
blank moments on the
pavement were methods.
I was afraid for the
future, afraid of the
unknown, sometimes
fear needs no reasons
or at least none that
we can ever know.
In spite of everything,
my situation, the fear,
how people looked
at me and the state of
the world, in spite of

all of it, there seemed
to be something deeply
therapeutic about
watching people's feet
as they passed me by.

Beaten

I had been on
the streets for
four and a half
months when
it happened.
I went to sleep
one night and
woke sometime
later in hospital
with the police
waiting at the
bottom of my
bed for me to waken.
I found out that
while I was asleep
on the street I was
attacked by two
men who partially
cut my throat,
fractured my jaw
and smashed the
back of my skull.
I was unconscious
for a whole day.

When I came around
the police wanted a
statement about what
had happened to me
but all I could tell them
was that they knew
more about it than I did.

What Is Homelessness?

What do you think
homeless people look,
act and think like?
Are they all addicted
and mentally unstable?
Are they all unhygienic?
I have always looked
after my appearance,
I have no addictions
and I have never lost
my mind but I have
been made homeless.
After a relationship
breakdown I had
nowhere to live. It
didn't matter how I
looked or thought
or even how I felt,
I simply had no home.
Do you have perceptions
about people who you
have never even met?
What is homelessness?

If more people asked themselves these questions the world would be a very different place.

Intimidation

In early spring,
I had only been
Homeless for a few
weeks and I was
sleeping in a park.
I had no problems
until very early
one Sunday morning.
I was woken abruptly
by a menacing voice
shouting, "Get the fuck
out of our park you
useless tramp!" It was
a group of wild-eyed
teenagers who were
drugged up and angry.
I gathered all my
possessions quickly,
thankful that they had
shouted first and
not just attacked me.
After that I learned
to avoid most people,
fear will do that to you.

Ageism

From the age
of fifteen I had
always worked.
At times I may
have had a week
or two without
work, between jobs,
but as I neared my
sixtieth birthday
potential employers
were telling me that
they were looking
for younger people.
Eventually my money
ran out and because
of pride I wouldn't
ask for help or apply
for state benefits.
I was shocked at what
had happened to me.

I had always worked
and paid my own way,
yet I was made homeless
simply because people
deemed me too old
to work.

Faith Restored

It was winter.
I found a shed on
a property that I
thought was empty
to sleep in overnight.
Early the next morning
I woke to an elderly
man prodding me
cautiously with
his walking stick.
I apologised and
was about to leave
but he invited me
into his house and
made me coffee.
His wife made us
bacon rolls and they
sat talking to me.
They asked about
the situation I was
in and I told them the
tolerable version of
my often twisted life.

After all I had been
through I didn't trust
people. I was paranoid
and overcautious but
the kindness that old
couple showed me stayed
with me and made me
realise that there were
still decent people in
this seemingly cruel world.

Home?

I was drinking
daily for years
and had been
close to death
more than once
when I found my
way to the hostel
in the big city.
As they were filling
out my details
upon admission,
I told them that if
I didn't get out of
my home town I
would probably die
a chemical death.
The woman dealing
with me asked me
where I had lived
and I had to pause.
With a mind full of
years of madness I
could not comprehend

that simple question.
Then she asked, "Where
do you call home?"
I remained silent for
a moment before
spluttering, "I don't
know if I have ever
had a home."

A Journey

I had been sleeping
rough in the big city
for three or four months
when a friend came to
me with the opportunity
of a job in a small town
seventy miles away.
We took all the money
we had and spent it on
travel but our contact
wouldn't answer his phone,
meaning our journey was
wasted and the job we
went for never happened.
We couldn't afford to get
the train back so we
decided to walk, and walk
we did, seventy miles along
the 'A' roads, stopping off
in towns along the way.
Our journey took six days.
Luckily it was summer.

Fists

I had a habit
of tucking my
fisted hands
under my head
while sleeping.
One winter's
morning I woke
to find both my
hands solidly
frozen into fists.
I couldn't move
my fingers so I
rubbed them on
my chest and
waited until I
could use them.
When I realised
later that it had
been minus nine
that night I was
thankful for
my bobble hat.

Without that it
could easily have
been my head
that had frozen up.

Starving

During the spring
we would sit by
the canal watching
the barges passing.
We were starving
but I noticed how
people would get
free samples at the
local market stalls.
I told my friend
about it and we would
go there smartened
up as best we could.
Standing near some
of the stalls I would
exclaim, "Well I don't
know what it tastes
like, do I!" The people
on the stalls would
hear us and offer us
bits of free food.

We would be doing
this at every second
or third stall and
soon we would not
be starving any more.

Good Samaritan

I had been on and
off the streets for
seven difficult years.
Struggling and
worrying, sleeping
on couches when
I was allowed to.
Wandering the
pavements, never
being able to settle.
One day as I walked
to my *Big Issue*
spot, I found a tenner
then further along
the road a packet of
cigarettes, a lucky day.
As I stood selling the
Big Issue, a clean-cut
man with an amazing
smile walked up to me.
He handed me a pile
of notes, £600 in all,
then he just walked
away again, I have
not seen him since.

I used that money to
get myself off the
streets, a little money
can change everything.

Overdose

He was deaf
and some people
in our company
would mock him.
I stuck up for him
because it was unfair.
We were shooting up
together and I grew
to like him over time.
One night he went
unconscious, it was
an overdose, I had
seen it happen before.
I used resuscitation
techniques and was
able to bring him back.
Saving a life is the
strangest feeling.
Later, after more drugs,
he overdosed again
but I wasn't there.
I went to the hospital
but he had already died.

I never knew his real name, I only knew him as Billabong.

Book by Cover

I wasn't street
homeless but I
was sleeping on
sofas and struggling
with my finances.
I had always taken
care of myself and
my appearance, no
matter how bad it got.
I thought it important
to hold onto my dignity.
One day in town, I was
stopped by a saleswoman,
she wanted me to buy
a cable TV package.
I kindly refused but she
was insistent and I had
to refuse again before
she asked me where I
lived to which I replied
"I am homeless."
She looked me up
and down and with a
smile that conveyed
disbelief she shook her

head and uttered a very
suspicious: "No!"
As I continued on an
old saying about books
and covers came to mind.

Collectively

One of the most
divisive aspects of
modern life comes
about because too
many people are
too comfortable.
Comfort causes
complacency, it
makes people think
everything is easy.
They look upon other
people's misfortune
as an individual,
personal failure
rather than as a
collective social
disaster. It's easier
to blame a small
group of people
than to admit that
our whole way
of life is causing
society's difficulties.

Motivation

After months
on the streets
I met a man
who I knew
from my life
of comfort, a
life long gone.
We used to
move in the
same worthy
circles but he
felt bad upon
seeing me and
seeing the state
I had become.
He gave me £40
out of some
strange sense
of unintentional
guilt. A few days
later I was having
an emotional episode
when I was comforted
by a fellow homeless
man who gave me

all the money he had,
around five pounds.
A person's social
standing and their
motivation can make
amounts irrelevant.

Cursing

Everything started
with an affair.
I was successful
as a husband,
as a father,
as a businessman.
I wanted for
nothing and my
life appeared perfect.
My wife was
divorcing me but
she manipulated me
into signing everything
over to her to prove
my love for her.
She got the business,
the house and all
of my assets, then
she cut me off and
left me with nothing.
What is the difference
between justice and
revenge? I couldn't

see my children and
that was the hardest
thing I have ever known.
In the space of a year
I went from being
worth a million to
living in a homeless
hostel and having
absolutely nothing.
I walked the streets
cursing my luck,
cursing my life,
cursing my ex-wife
but mostly cursing
myself.

Foraging

I was sleeping
out in the woods.
I enjoyed camping
when I was young
but it was different
when I was homeless.
I got a book about
foraging and I took
to finding berries
and eatable plants
and mushrooms.
I laughed to myself
that I was picking
mushrooms to stop
myself from starving
rather than to get high.
I didn't always need
to forage but out of
necessity sometimes
I would have to.
Even though life was
tough living in the
woods it was good to

know that I could
survive by myself
if I needed to.

Moved On

When a group of us
gathered somewhere
the police would often
come and move us on.
Even though we
had nowhere to go,
they moved us on.
Being on the street
was bad enough but
being constantly
harassed by the
police for being
on the street was
difficult to take.
One night we were
moved on and we
ended up in a park
in the city only for
the police to come
again, at two in the
morning, and move
us on, only this time
with water cannons.

Pride

I left home and
was living on
the city streets
far from my home.
Because I didn't
want people to
know how bad
my life had become
I told everyone
that I had a job,
I was doing well.
One Christmas, my
mother and father
came shopping in
the city and when
I met them my
mother took one
look at me and said
"You don't really
have a job, do you?"
Pride can be destructive
and though you may

be able to keep things
from yourself, you
can't always keep it
from everyone else.

Invisible

As I sat on my
sleeping bag
each day on
the same street,
I watched the
world persisting.
Most people just
ignored me and I
didn't blame them,
I understood that
because I wished
I could have ignored
myself at times.
It's not that I wanted
to be noticed but
there is something
about being overlooked
by hundreds of people
every day that makes
you begin to feel
invisible.

Timely

After one week
of homelessness,
I was sleeping
near some woods
at the edge of
playing fields.
I woke one morning
to a soaked pungent
smell and caught
the last of a fox
disappearing through
the hedge after it
had marked me as
part of its territory.
Since I was drinking
and drugging heavily
my emotional state
was fraught at best.
I felt at that moment
that I had had enough.
As I looked at
the nearby railway
lines, I ruminated
going on a journey.

I was crying when
very suddenly a
black cat came from
nowhere, jumped up
on my lap and sat
there staring at me.
At times the strangest
things can happen at
just the right time to
shift your perspective.

Life

A friend who
I looked out
for, out on the
streets, suddenly
went missing.
I asked around
and looked for
him and eventually
mutual friends told
me that he didn't
want to see me but
they didn't know why.
When I found him
he had a bandanna
around his throat
and all of his teeth
were missing.
He had been left
a lot of money by
his grandmother
and at the same
time contracted
cancer of the throat.

He was dead within
a couple of months.
Life can be cruel
sometimes and
sometimes it can
be kind and sometimes
it can be cruel
and kind all at once.

A Bowl of Noodles

It was a beautiful
summer evening
and I was dozing
on a park bench.
I awoke being gently
nudged by a woman
holding a steaming
bowl of noodles.
It was unexpected
and because the area
was quite secluded
I couldn't figure out
where she'd come
from until she pointed
up to her flat saying
she'd seen me from
her window while
she was making the
meal for herself.
She sat with me for
a time talking as
I ate her noodles.
Sometimes life can be
good even when it isn't.

Facing Myself

When I was 14
my mother threw
me out and made
me homeless.
I eventually went
and lived with a
friend's family
but I was never
really settled,
I never quite got
over being rejected
by my mother.
I used alcohol and
drugs so I wouldn't
have to face myself
and I wasted years
upsetting people and
making life very
difficult for myself.
I was difficult to
live with so I became
homeless again.

Looking back now
I can understand why
people were upset
with me and I can
also understand that
it was the alcohol
and drugs that stopped
me from honestly
facing my inner self.

The Bed

I had been out
on the streets
for months,
sleeping in
parks and in
woods and
anywhere I
was able to
hide myself
to feel safe.
A group of
squatters asked
me to come
and live with
them in an
abandoned
nursing home.
I had electricity
and my own
room and I
even had a bed.
I was amazed
by that bed.

I hadn't slept
in a bed for
six months.
Those first
nights in that
bed made me
think about how
we take for
granted things
that we should
be grateful for.

The Red Book

At the beginning
of my homelessness
I would listen to the
old men who had
been on the streets
for years. I would
meet them in hostels,
day centres and
in parks, they told
me about where
you could get food.
In a little red book
I compiled a database
of places, times, days
and of organisations,
churches and people
who distributed food.
I kept that book,
I still have it!
That little red book
meant that even
though life was tough
at least I wasn't going
to starve.

Yellow

After a lifetime
of alcohol and
drugs and the
emotional madness
which that brought
I became rational
enough to seek help.
I was living in a
hostel, getting support
and I was teaching
myself sanity again.
Music had always
been my passion and
I would busk for
the love of it
on the streets.
One winters evening
I was playing the
song 'Yellow' when
a group of drunk
students attacked me.
I was badly beaten
for no reason.

My face was black and
purple, ribs broken,
I was hospitalised.
I lapsed from recovery
and my life began
spiralling madly
downwards once more,
Somehow though I
began climbing back up.
I met a beautiful
woman and fell in
love and the past
seemed so far away
but I can never
forget the sadness
of the song Yellow.

Contrasts

There I was,
surrounded by
diplomats and
dignitaries, VIPs
and royalty, at
the 25th anniversary
of Emmaus UK in
the French embassy
in central London.
I took great pleasure
in telling the assembled
guests that I had been
living not far away
in Hyde Park for
a year and a half.
I had been homeless
for a long time when
I went through serious
doubt and despair
and depression, yet
here I was speaking
confidently to these
amazing people and
shaking hands with the
Duchess of Cornwall.

No matter how bad it
gets it can always be
worse and no matter
how bad it gets it can
always eventually
get better.

Present and Past

About two weeks
before Christmas,
I was sleeping
on a friend's sofa.
I was conscious
of disturbing my
friend and his
girlfriend so I would
stay away as long
as possible before
going to their house.
I walked around
with nowhere to go.
It was December,
I noticed strangers and
how they were enjoying
the Christmas season.
At first I felt sad, but
then I began remembering
my past and how I used
to enjoy Christmas
with my loving family,
the privilege I had once.
In one sense I missed my
old life, but in another

I was distantly happy
for these strangers.
I sat by the river with
mixed feelings waiting
for some time to pass.

Why?

I don't know why
I was homeless,
I shouldn't have been.
I came from relative
comfort and when
I went onto the street
I was shocked that
people really lived
like that, I may have
been naïve in ways.
Maybe I was following
some vague instinct or
maybe I didn't care,
it felt like I didn't care.
I didn't beg or drink
or drug excessively
but I still went around
with homeless people.
Was it a lifestyle choice?
I may not have been
ready for it to get better
while it was happening.

I think I just accepted
it and felt I couldn't
do anything about it
right then but I knew
eventually it would get
better and eventually it
did get better, eventually.
I moved on, life got
easier, I have a job and
a home and a purpose
in life but even now
I still don't know why
I was homeless, perhaps
I never will know why.

Ten Pence

Trying to avoid
the very idea of
people lead me
to search out
rural retreats.
I found a bridge
with an overhang
that I covered with
a tarpaulin creating
a little comfort
amid my discomfort.
I was teaching myself
the tin whistle and
though I wasn't very
good at the beginning
I continued trying.
As I played one day
a little man surprised
me when he appeared
and he stood there in
the middle of nowhere
listening to me play.
"Are you busking?"

he asked me. "I will,"
I said, "but I have only
started learning it."
He gave me the first
money I earned for
busking, it was only
ten pence but it was
a surreal experience
because as soon as he
had arrived he was gone.
Afterwards I wondered
if it meant anything.

Attempted Murder

I was sheltering in
a park, keeping out
of the rain under the
canopy of a building.
At around midnight
I fell fast asleep.
At some time after
two I woke abruptly
to find the bottom of
my sleeping bag
was blazing flames.
I quickly got out of
it and I wasn't burned,
but the person who had
set me alight was gone.
I sat there shocked at
what had happened
wondering why someone
would want to set a
complete stranger on
fire for no apparent reason.

My Old Boots

I don't often wear
my old boots but
when I do I think
back to my years
of nothingness.
I slept in these boots,
worked in them
and lived, socialised.
For three years
I wore these boots
and even though all
that ended three years
ago I haven't been able
to throw them away.
Behind my door
is the old coat I
wore with them,
I couldn't throw
that away either.
I don't know why.
There's a strange
sentimentality with
these old boots and
that scruffy old coat.

Appreciation

There was a
reverend whose
church was on
the road that
I spent time on
while I was
living on the street.
He used to bring
me food and sit
with me, he always
had time for me.
Often, after his
congregation had
gone home, he would
bring me in out of
the rain and we
would talk for hours.
He told me everything
would eventually get
better for me, he always
said that and he was
right because everything
did get better for me.

I don't see him much
now but we're still in
touch and I still tell
him how much I appreciate
everything he did for me.

A Choice?

Many of us believe
that the homeless
are solely responsible
for their lives and
the situations they
find themselves in.
Even though people
need to learn to be
responsible for their
actions there is a
difference between
making a choice and
not having a choice.
Do you really think
that someone would
choose homelessness?
Like there was an option
between the streets and
a nice easy quiet life
and they've decided:
"Well no, I think I'll
live on the street, thanks!"

If you see homelessness
as simply the failure of
certain wayward individuals
then you have a very
limited understanding of how
a modern society functions.
There is a fear that if we
show compassion to the
homeless we will somehow
make things worse but when
will we begin to consider
that there is a difference
between understanding
something and condoning it?

Familiar

I would sit on
the street outside
a train-station
and seeing certain
commuters daily
made their presence
strangely familiar.
You can get used to
people without even
knowing them by
sharing smiles and
nods with them over
many, many weeks.
A familiar face came
to me one morning
and offered me money.
I wasn't begging though,
I was just sitting there
so I told him I didn't
want money but if he
wanted he could get
me some food instead.

Moments later he came
back to me with some
pasties then we shared
a smile and a nod and
off he went to work.

Underpass

I had tried sleeping
in the centre of
the city but a
combination of
party people, bin
lorries and constant
urban decibels made
quiet almost impossible.
I went away, out to the
outskirts and found a
dry underpass amid
the motorway sprawl.
There was less traffic
at night and when
I put my head down,
the gentle bump, bump...
bump, bump...
bump, bump of cars
passing on the road
above, yards from my
face made a peaceful
rhythm that would
always send me to sleep.

Fish and Chips

I was hungry,
I was tired,
I was freezing.
I was waiting
for people to
put enough into
my plastic cup
so I could buy
fish and chips.
Four lads walked
passed me, dressed
in material privilege,
drunkenly happy.
One was going to
put money into
my cup when his
friend said, "Don't
give them money,
they'll just drink it."
The lad hesitated
and he asked me,
"Will you drink it?"
"I don't drink!"

I told him,
"I just want fish
and chips."

Wandering

I have always
been a loner,
I don't know why.
I am not sure
if it's a choice.
I have always
been a wanderer,
never able to settle,
moving from town
to town from
country to country.
I would just up and
go, never thinking,
never looking back.
I am only young
but this is how my
life has always been,
this wandering and
not knowing why,
never able to settle.

I am getting sick of
this transient lifestyle
and part of me wants
to stop but I don't
know when and I
don't know where.

Stashed

Because I moved
around so much
I took to keeping
little stashes of
essentials hidden
from town to town.
Some food, some drink,
gloves and hats and
socks and anything
else I might need.
I would put everything
in a sleeping bag then
roll it up and hide it.
I walked a long way
one night and went
to one of my stashes
and when I opened it
up I realised that
someone had found
it and took a shit in it.
I was disgusted and
very angry. I waited
there, hidden, I was
seething, more than a
day I waited for them

but they didn't return.
When eventually I left
part of me was glad they
didn't come back because
if they had I probably
would have hurt someone.

Redundant

I had a normal
life, a job I liked,
a partner, a child.
Suddenly I was
made redundant
and everything
changed, fast.
I couldn't get
another job and
when I ended up
being short on my
mortgage payment
they showed no
patience and our house
was repossessed.
My wife and I
split up shortly after
and I ended up in
a homeless hostel.
I had always worked
and had never been
homeless before that.
It took just over one
month for my life to
fall completely apart.

Gherkins

I used to sleep
in a graveyard
trying to hide
from the world
and from myself.
One night after
the pubs closed,
some drunk kids
came by. I was
going to leave
but they asked
me to stay and
we sat talking
through the night.
They wanted to
know about me,
about my homeless
life. They cared,
those drunk kids
cared more than
most people did.
One of them got
up and said he'd
be back in a minute.

Sometime later he
returned with food
for me including
the biggest jar of
chip shop gherkins.
I was so thankful
I was nearly crying,
but in the back of my
mind I was thinking,
"How am I going to
carry these around?"

Candles

I liked the
darkness.
I always looked
for places away
from light and
I would sit for
hours in front
of a candle
watching my
shadow flickering
on the wall.
Most people
don't like darkness
but sitting in
the darkness with
my candles used
to give me such
a peaceful feeling.

Culmination

When I was five
or six, my mother
left and I didn't
see her for years.
My father was a
heroin addict so I
grew up surrounded
by drug users and
heavy drinkers.
By the time I got
to my early twenties
I was using cocaine
daily and because
of the crowd I was
mixing with, I became
homeless and had to
leave my hometown.
When I was growing
up and during my drug
use, I didn't know I had
choices, my mind was
so clouded that my
choices seemed limited.

If I had known myself better and had a better start, I am sure my life would not have been the chaotic mess it became.

Pressing the Button

My whole life
I was pressing
the button.
I don't know why.
I couldn't settle.
My life was a
constant cycle of
alcohol and anger
but since I was
self-conscious and
sensitive I tended
not to seek help or
even look at myself.
I went up and down
in a chaotic existence.
Losing jobs, being
evicted, drinking and
ending up on the street.
It went on for 30 years.
At some point, around
the age of 50, I stopped
pressing that button.
I don't know why.

Maybe I had learned
enough to help myself
or maybe I just grew
tired of all the chaos.

The Kind Man

One night, a man
who looked kind
came and sat with
me on the pavement.
Usually people just
ignored me so when
someone bothered to
come and speak to me
I really appreciated it.
He gave me twenty
pounds, he gave me his
phone number as well.
We have stayed in touch.
He was pleased for me
when I got into an
Emmaus community
and my life improved.
He sends me positive
text messages that
always cheer me up.
He lives away across
the sea and he said that
someday I can go and
visit him, I hope I will
be able to that sometime.

Unexpected

My life wasn't
perfect but it
was comfortable.
I was married,
I worked hard,
I had much more
than I needed.
Suddenly though,
I had a stroke and
was hospitalised
for three months.
When it came time
for my discharge
my wife no longer
wanted me because
I wasn't going to
be able to work.
I had nothing and
nowhere to go so
I was thankful when
I found Emmaus.
I was grateful to
have a place to stay
and food, warmth
and relative comfort.

Sometimes life can
take unexpected turns
but I don't know what
I would have done
if Emmaus had not
been there to help me.

Sorry

A friend and
I slept in the
porch of a church.
Most of the time
it was quiet but
one night I heard
voices coming
up the graveyard.
It was two lads
acting suspiciously,
I could tell that they
were out for trouble.
One kicked out at me
but I was able to get
up and out of my
open sleeping bag
very quickly.
They were shocked
when I stood up
because I am 6"4,
and after their faces
dropped they sprinted.

Later when we woke
up there were a couple
of coffees, a fiver and
a note that said sorry.

Too Comfortable

I never wanted to
get too comfortable.
I think it came from
what I was used to,
it was never a choice.
I still feel that way
and many people don't
understand my thinking.
Real comfort for me is
earning what you've
got and not expecting
more than you deserve.
There is a risk I will
end up revisiting
the madness of my
scattered past if
I get too comfortable.
I cannot allow that to
happen, I stop myself
from becoming too
comfortable, I would
much rather just be
comfortable enough.

Comfortable?

I was out there
so long, so many
years spent living
like a wild animal,
it became normal.
Eventually I got help
and found my way to
an Emmaus community,
but the comfort and
love and normality
was something I was
not accustomed to.
In my room, I kept
my old rucksack
and sleeping bag
that I had with me
out on the streets.
Every now and then
I would take out the
sleeping bag and
sleep in it on the floor.
Physical comfort and
mental comfort is not
always as precise as
people may believe.

Swapsies

My friend would
often beg outside
a night club in town,
you could make a
few quid doing that.
I went to see him
one night as he was
talking to a reveller.
I thought something
was wrong at first
but soon realised that
the man was refused
entry because he was
wearing tracksuit bottoms."
He was trying to talk
my pal into doing a part
exchange, his old jeans
for the tracksuit bottoms
and a crisp ten-pound note.
My friend didn't want to
go for it but I made him
realise that a tenner was
more important than an
old pair of scruffy jeans.

The deal was done, they
swapped clothes in an
alleyway, the tenner
was handed over then
off went the reveller,
clubbing in a homeless
person's filthy trousers.
I was laughing while it
was happening because
it was so absurd and
even now when I think
back to it from all these
years away I can't help
but laugh about it.

A Hot Shower

After months on
the streets my
first hot shower
on my first
night in Emmaus
was something
I will never forget.
I stood there for
ages sighing as
the steaming water
made me tingle.
Sometimes we
get so comfortable
that we take all
in life for granted.
But that first shower
and climbing into
a clean, warm bed
felt like the
most blissful
moments of my life.

Strength

The second time
I met Abbé Pierre
was a few years
before he died.
He was in a
wheelchair.
Despite the fact
that he was old
and frail he still
had an undeniable
energy that he gave
to anyone who so
much as looked at him.
As he was being
pushed past a group
of us he stopped for
just a moment and
his eyes caught mine.
He gave me a great
big smile then
clenched both his
fists and put them
up to me to indicate
I needed to be strong.

Then on he went,
leaving me with a
most enduring memory.

The Author

Séamus Fox was born in Belfast and brought up in Craigavon. He has been writing since his mid-teens in many different formats and was very active in Belfast especially from around 2007, mostly with spoken word and occasionally comedy. In 2009 he won the All Ireland Slam in Galway and he published his first book, *As Seen Through Staggered Eyes*, the following year.

Having experienced the absolute horror of alcoholism and the arduous task of getting sober he realised the power of writing as a tool for understanding and changing. In late 2015 he moved to London to find work and after several months he found himself homeless. Séamus has been completely sober for more than 7 years and he has noticed a massive change in how he sees the world as a result of sobriety.

Eventually he found Emmaus and he now works and lives at the Cambridge Community. He undertook the writing of this book to give something back to the Emmaus family that he feels such a part of, but also to raise awareness about the serious social issues surrounding homelessness and addiction.

Emmaus in the UK

There are currently 29 Emmaus communities open in the UK, with four groups looking to establish new communities in their area. Here's where you can find us

1. CAMBRIDGE
2. COVENTRY
3. GREENWICH
4. DOVER
5. MOSSLEY
6. BRIGHTON & HOVE
7. GLOUCESTERSHIRE
8. HERTFORDSHIRE
9. VILLAGE CARLTON
10. LEEDS
11. BRISTOL
12. BOLTON
13. GLASGOW
14. LAMBETH
15. COLCHESTER
16. SHEFFIELD
17. PRESTON
18. HAMPSHIRE
19. OXFORD
20. BURNLEY
21. NORFOLK & WAVENEY
22. HASTINGS & ROTHER
23. MEDWAY
24. LEICESTERSHIRE & RUTLAND
25. SALFORD
26. SOUTH WALES
27. HULL & EAST RIDING
28. MERSEYSIDE
29. NORTH EAST

A. SUFFOLK
B. BRADFORD
C. POTTERIES
D. CORNWALL

Emmaus UK Unit 302 Scott House The Custard Factory Gibb Street Birmingham B9 4AA
t 0300 303 7555 www.emmaus.org.uk

Emmaus UK is a registered charity number 1064470 and company limited by guarantee number 3422341, registered in England and Wales

#0001 - 070818 - C2 - 203/127/8 - PB - 9781912092550